The Nature Kid's Guide to

PHEASANTS

DAVID ANDERSON

LP Media Inc. Publishing

For information address LP Media Inc. Publishing,
30012 Variolite St NW, Princeton MN 55371
www.lpmedia.org

Publication Data

Pheasants
The Nature Kid's Guide to Pheasants — First edition.

Summary: "Learn all about Pheasants, the Nature Kid Way"
— Provided by publisher.

ISBN: 979-8-89818-243-4

[1. Pheasants – Non-Fiction] I. Title.

Title: The Nature Kid's Guide to Pheasants

CONTENTS

PRAIRIE HOMES

Ring-necked pheasants can run up to 10 miles per hour — almost as fast as you can sprint!

Crow! A bright rooster calls across a wide grassy field.

A flash of copper and green bursts from the tall grass. A ring-necked pheasant is on the move — and it looks like it has always belonged here. But this bird is actually a newcomer with a remarkable story.

Ring-necked pheasants came from Asia. People brought them to North America in the 1880s, hoping they would thrive as a game bird. Nobody expected just how well that would go.

Open farmland and tall prairie grass turned out to be exactly what they needed. But the ring-neck is just one of dozens of spectacular pheasant species found around the world.

FEATHERED FLASHERS

A rooster's feathers have over 20 different colors — more than a box of crayons!

Puff! A rooster fluffs his feathers and glows like a rainbow.

Male pheasants are very colorful. They have green heads and red face patches. A white ring wraps around the neck, giving them their name. Their copper and gold feathers shine in the sun.

Hens look very different. Their brown feathers blend in with grass and dirt. This **camouflage** keeps them safe from predators while they sit on nests.

Colors tell a story in nature. A bright rooster shows he is strong and healthy. Hens pick the most colorful males to be their mates.

EXPLOSIVE ESCAPE
FUN FACT!
A flushing pheasant can reach 40 miles per hour in just a few wingbeats!
8

Whoosh! A pheasant bursts from the grass like a rocket!

Pheasants hide in tall grass most of the time. They stay very still so predators walk right past. But when danger gets close, they burst into the air!

This sudden burst is called a **flush**. Their wings beat fast and loud. The noise can scare a fox or hawk, giving the bird time to escape.

Pheasants do not fly far, though. They flap hard, glide low, and drop back down. Then they hide in the grass again, waiting for the next threat to pass.

STAY BACK!

A rooster's crow can be heard from half a mile away!

Squawk! A rooster flaps his wings and crows to claim his turf.

Each rooster guards a patch of land in spring. He crows loudly to tell other males to stay away. Then he flaps his wings to look big and strong.

If another rooster comes too close, a fight may start. The birds kick and peck at each other. Sharp **spurs** on their legs can cause real damage. The winner gets to keep the territory.

A rooster with good land attracts the most hens. Many hens may join him in his space. He struts and shows off his bright feathers to impress them all.

HUNGRY BIRDS

Scratch, scratch! A pheasant digs through leaves for seeds.

Pheasants spend most of their day on the ground. They walk through fields and scratch the dirt for food. Their strong feet are made for digging.

These birds eat seeds, grains, and bugs. In summer, they munch on grasshoppers and beetles. In fall, they search for corn and wheat left behind after harvest.

Pheasants also need cover to stay safe. Thick grass and weedy patches give them places to rest and hide. Without these spots, foxes and hawks would find them easily.

INVISIBLE HENS

A sitting hen is so well camouflaged that researchers have accidentally stepped within inches of one without seeing her!

Shhh! A hen pheasant blends in with the tall grass.

While the rooster gets all the attention, the hen pheasant is built for something even more important — survival. Her brown, streaked feathers blend so perfectly into dry grass and dead leaves that she can disappear in plain sight. Standing just a few feet away, most **predators** walk right past her.

Hens are also much smaller and quieter than roosters. No bright colors, no loud crowing, no flashy displays. Everything about a hen is designed to stay hidden and keep her eggs safe.

That dull brown coat is one of the most effective camouflage patterns in the bird world.

WINTER WARRIORS

Pheasants can survive temperatures as cold as 30 degrees below zero — way colder than your freezer!

Brr! A pheasant digs through deep snow to find food.

Winter can be hard for pheasants. Cold wind and deep snow hide their food. Many birds move to thick brush and weedy spots for shelter.

Pheasants huddle in groups to stay warm. They fluff their feathers to trap heat close to their bodies. On the coldest nights, they dig into the snow. This blocks the icy wind.

Food can be hard to find. Pheasants scratch through snow to reach seeds and grain. Farmers help by leaving old crops standing, which gives pheasants food all winter long.

HUNTING HELPERS

Woof! A hunting dog flushes a rooster pheasant on a cold fall morning.

People have hunted pheasants for hundreds of years. In many states, pheasant season is a big fall event. Hunters use dogs to flush the birds from tall grass.

Hunting money helps pheasants, too. Some of it pays to create new **habitat**. Groups plant grassy fields and wetlands where pheasants can thrive.

Pheasants also need help from farmers. Leaving strips of grass by crop fields makes a big difference. Pheasants use these strips to nest, raise chicks, and hide from predators.

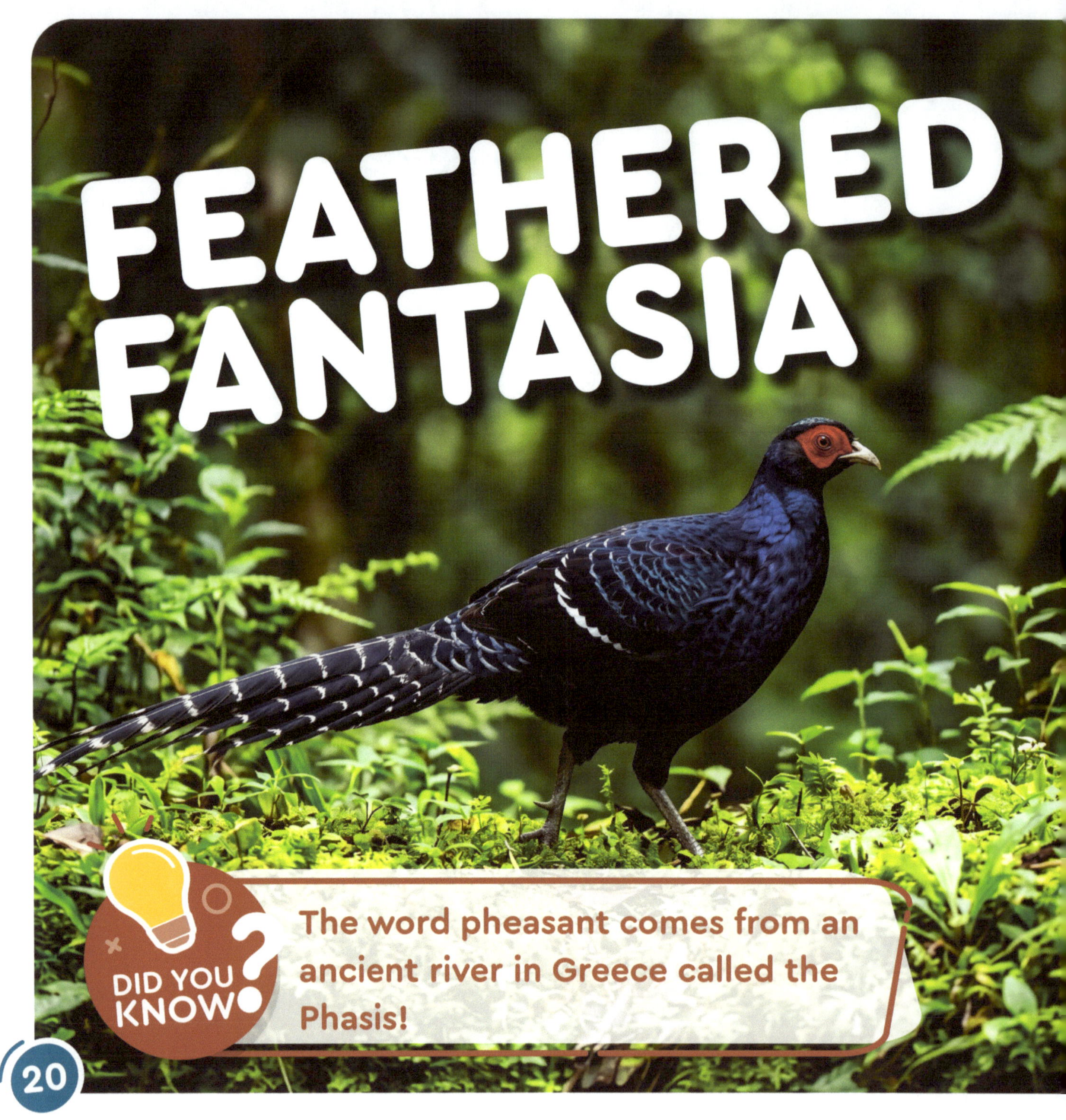

FEATHERED FANTASIA

DID YOU KNOW?

The word pheasant comes from an ancient river in Greece called the Phasis!

Cluck! A mikado pheasant calls out in a thick jungle far from any farm.

There are over fifty kinds of pheasants! They live across Asia and beyond. You can find them in forests, mountains, and steamy jungles. Each kind looks and acts in its own special way.

Some have tails longer than your bed. Others have feathers that glow like jewels. A few are so rare that almost no one has ever seen them in the wild.

Get ready to meet some of the most amazing pheasants on Earth. Each one will surprise you.

GOLDEN GLORY

A golden pheasant can run through thick brush faster than it can fly!

Swoosh! A flash of gold and red darts through a dark forest.

Golden pheasants live in the mountain forests of China. Males have golden crests, orange capes, and bright red bellies. They are some of the most colorful birds alive.

In spring, a male fans out his orange cape. It looks like a striped umbrella around his face! This flashy show helps him attract a mate.

Golden pheasants are shy and hard to spot. They stick to thick brush where they can hide from predators. Most people only see them in zoos or wildlife parks.

SCALED SPLENDOR

24

Rustle! A beautiful pheasant rests in the shade in a Chinese forest.

Lady Amherst's pheasant is one of the fanciest birds alive. The male has a long silvery tail and a cape of black and white feathers. Each feather looks like a tiny fish scale.

This bird lives in thick bamboo forests in China. It likes to stay hidden in the shadows and is very hard to find in the wild.

Lady Amherst was a real person. In the 1800s, she sent one of these birds to London. Scientists named the whole species after her.

MONAL MAGIC

DID YOU KNOW?
Himalayan monals live above 15,000 feet — higher than many airplanes fly!

Whir! A rainbow bird stands on a steep mountain slope.

The Himalayan monal is the national bird of Nepal. It lives high up in the mountains of South Asia, on grassy slopes and rocky cliffs.

The male shines like a living rainbow. His feathers glow green, purple, blue, and copper. When the sun hits him, the colors shift and change like magic.

Monals dig in the ground with their strong beaks. They pull up roots, bugs, and seeds from the soil. When winter comes, they move to lower slopes where food is easier to find.

LONG TAILS

FUN
FACT!

The longest Reeves's pheasant tail ever measured was over eight feet — longer than a car!

Swish! A tail longer than a grown-up stretches through the trees.

Reeves's pheasants have the longest tails in the bird world! A male's tail can grow over five feet long. That is taller than most second graders.

This bird lives in the forests of central China. It likes hilly woods with thick brush and spends its time walking the forest floor.

Sadly, Reeves's pheasants are losing their homes. People have cut down many forests where they live. Scientists are working hard to protect the forests that remain.

SILVER STRIPES
FUN FACT!
There are more than 15 different types of silver pheasant — each with slightly different markings!

Crunch! A silver and white bird steps through dry forest leaves.

Silver pheasants are large, graceful birds. The males have white feathers with thin black lines running down their backs. Their faces and legs are bright red.

These birds live in the forests of Southeast Asia. You can find them in China, Vietnam, and Thailand. They like to stay near streams and shady forest paths.

Silver pheasants are easier to spot than many wild pheasants. They are not as shy as some of their cousins. Small groups often walk together through the woods, searching for food.

JADE JEWELS

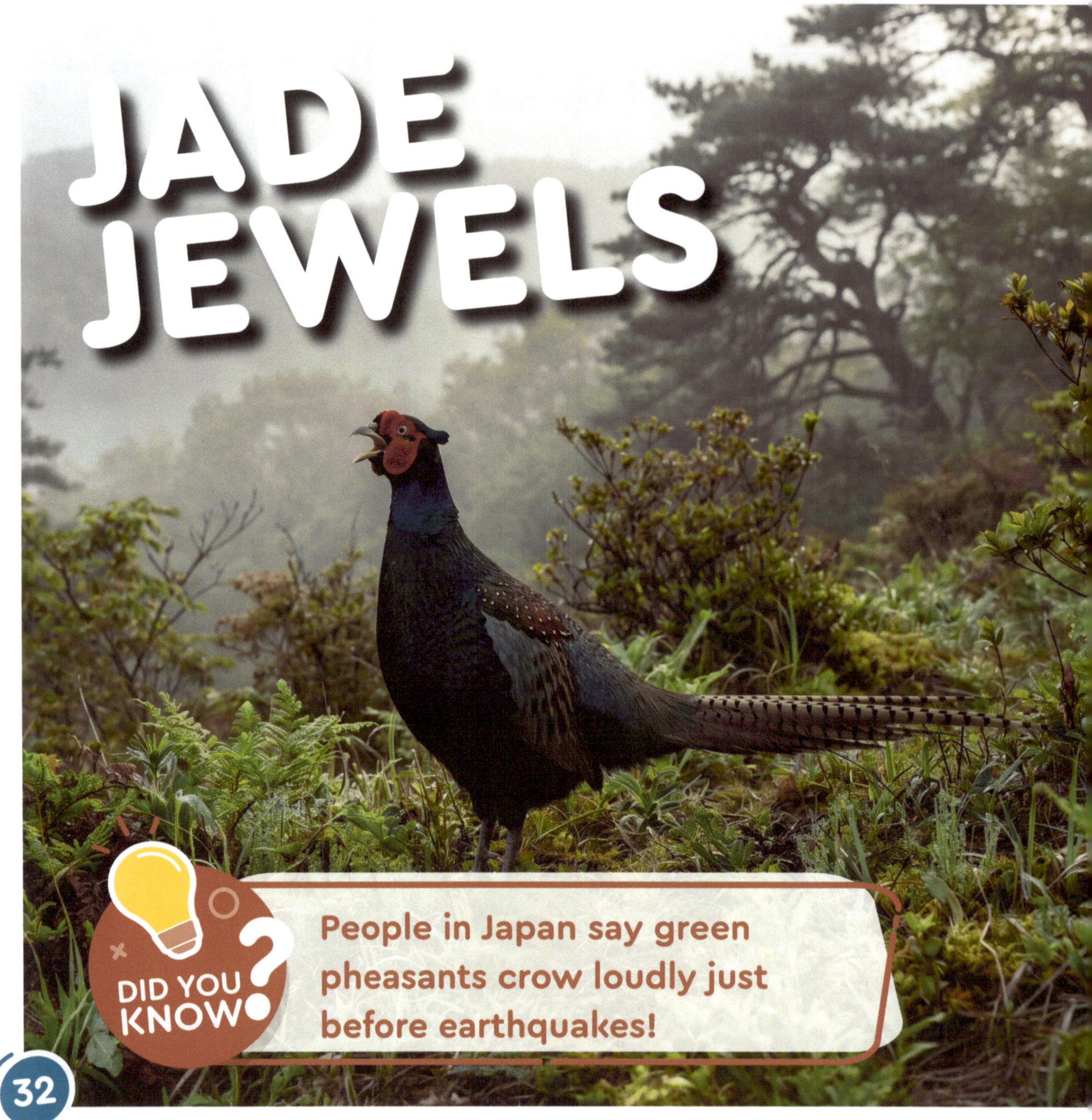

DID YOU KNOW?

People in Japan say green pheasants crow loudly just before earthquakes!

Kee-kee! A green pheasant calls from a misty Japanese hillside.

The green pheasant is the national bird of Japan. It is the only pheasant found wild in that country. Males have dark green chests and purple necks that shine in the light.

Green pheasants live in fields, forests, and even near towns. They are not very shy around people. You might spot one walking through a park or garden!

In Japan, the green pheasant appears in old stories and art. People there have loved this bird for hundreds of years. It is a symbol of courage and good luck.

EYES, EYES

The eye-spots on a peacock pheasant's tail can reflect light like tiny mirrors!

34

Flutter! Rows of glowing eye-spots flash on a fanned-out tail.

Peacock pheasants are small but beautiful birds. The males have shiny spots on their tails that look like tiny eyes. These spots glow blue and green, just like a peacock's tail.

These birds live in the rain forests of Southeast Asia. They walk quietly on the dark forest floor. Their small size helps them slip through thick plants without being seen.

To impress a female, the male spreads his tail wide. He tilts it toward the hen so she can see every glowing spot. It is like a tiny light show in the forest!

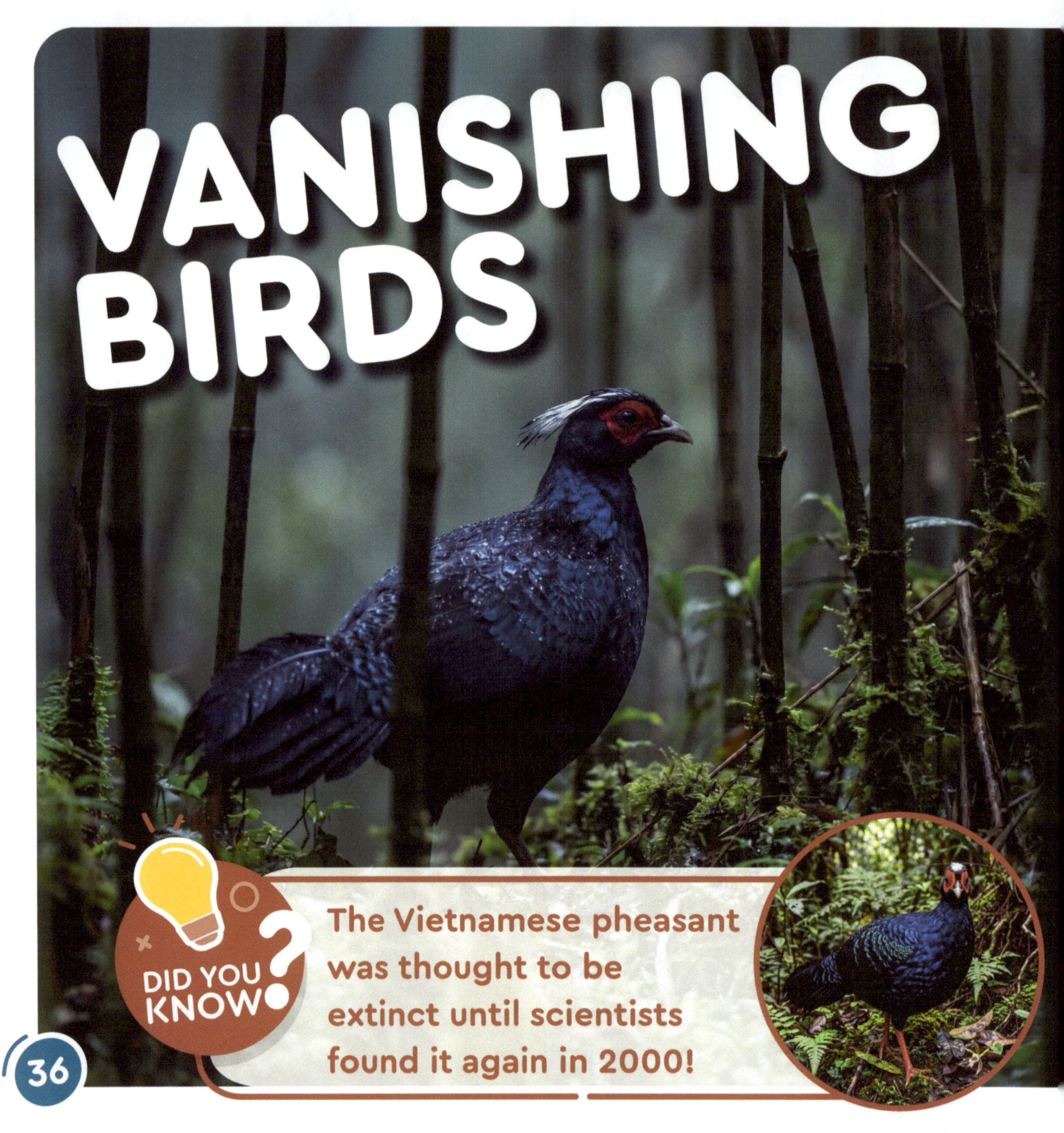

VANISHING BIRDS

The Vietnamese pheasant was thought to be extinct until scientists found it again in 2000!

Hush! Somewhere deep in the forest, a rare pheasant hides.

Some pheasants are in danger of dying out. Edwards's pheasant from Vietnam has almost vanished from the wild. Fewer than 100 may be left. Scientists did not see one in the wild for over 20 years!

Forests are being cut down all over Asia. When trees are lost, pheasants lose their homes and food. Some kinds have nowhere left to go.

Zoos and scientists are working to save these birds. They raise chicks and protect wild forests. Every single bird matters when a species is this rare.

FEATHERED SURPRISES

Chirp! A pheasant chick peeps as it runs through morning grass.

Most people know the ring-necked pheasant. But as you have seen, that is just the start. Some pheasants glow like rainbows. Some have tails longer than a grown adult. Others flash rows of glowing eye-spots like something from another world.

These birds live in forests and mountains across Asia, and many are rarely seen by people at all.

When we protect wild places, we protect the birds that live inside them. And some of those birds are among the most beautiful animals on Earth.

GLOSSARY

flush

When a bird bursts into the air suddenly from hiding.

predator

An animal that hunts and eats other animals.

camouflage

Colors or patterns that help an animal blend into its surroundings and hide.

habitat

The natural place where an animal lives and finds food.

spur

A sharp, pointed spike on a bird's leg used for fighting.